P9-BYM-602

PugTherapy

PugTherapy

Finding Happiness,
One Pug at a Time

Beverly West and Jason Bergund

Photographs by Jessica Alonso

BROADWAY BOOKS
New York

B
BROADWAY

PUBLISHED BY BROADWAY BOOKS

Copyright © 2006 by Beverly West, Jason Bergund, and Jessica Alonso

All Rights Reserved

Published in the United States by Broadway Books, an imprint of The Doubleday
Broadway Publishing Group, a division of Random House, Inc., New York.
www.broadwaybooks.com

BROADWAY BOOKS and its logo, a letter B bisected on the diagonal, are trademarks of
Random House, Inc.

Book design by Nicola Ferguson

Photographs by Jessica Alonso

Library of Congress Cataloging-in-Publication Data

West, Beverly, 1961–

Pugtherapy : finding happiness, one pug at a time /
Beverly West and Jason Bergund.—1st ed.

p. cm

(alk. paper)

1. Pug—Pictorial works. 2. Photography of dogs. I. Bergund, Jason. II. Title.

SF429.P9W47 2006

636.76—dc22   2005044872

ISBN-13: 978-0-7679-2204-3

ISBN-10: 0-7679-2204-2

PRINTED IN JAPAN

1 3 5 7 9 10 8 6 4 2

FIRST EDITION

To our grandparents,

who taught us how to talk to the
animals, especially Frances Milton,
a dear friend; and in loving
memory of Judson Miles Rees,
who had a zest for living, loving,
and learning, and Pat Holden, a
gentleman and a poet, who never
said no at the pet store.

PugTherapy

Introduction

PugTherapy is our pug family album, which illustrates what pugs and their owners have known for years: that pugs are more than just man's best friend—they're a form of therapy that can cure anything from a day in the doghouse to a full-fledged CAT-astrophe.

Whether life's got you on a short leash or you're feeling like a dog without a bone, the illustrated prescriptions in *PugTherapy* will help you find the comfort, inspiration, humor, and unconditional love we all need to reenter the puppy pageant of life and win Best in Show.

Our family of pure- and not-so-purebred pugs, caught in the act of just being themselves, reassures us all that even in a dog-eat-dog world,

every pug has its day—and reminds
us that happiness is as simple as re-
membering to count our blessings,
one pug at a time.

We all have days when we feel
like we're in the doghouse . . .

Or like we're stuck on the
outside, looking in . . .

. . . Or just a little dazed
and confused.

Even top dogs can get to feeling a
little low every once in a while.

But all you really need at times
like these is a little PugTherapy.

PugTherapy is easy, once you get
started. The first thing you have
to do is smile.

Remember to wear your heart
on your collar.

Pretty soon, you'll start to notice
all kinds of things to be happy
about—like bubble baths by
candlelight . . .

rocking chairs and
flowers . . .

the shade of
old apple trees . . .

romantic moments with
someone who makes your
heart go pitter-patter . . .

. . . and ripe berries with
lots of cream.

In fact, once you start to get
the hang of PugTherapy, you'll
discover all kinds of ways to turn
your bars . . .

. . . into stars.

When you're feeling bored with
the banquet of life . . .

try out a new recipe . . .

. . . Or make a new friend.

If you're feeling fenced in . . .

run through
"The Gates" . . .

Climb to the top of a hill
and watch the snow fall . . .

go for a drive . . .

take a road trip
with a friend . . .

. . . Or have a picnic.

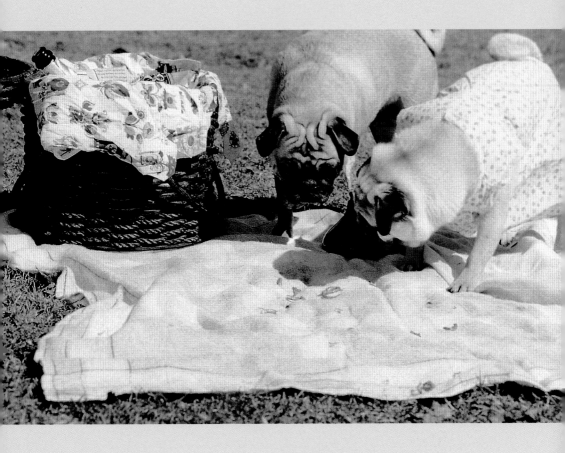

If you're having a bad hair day…

try on a new hat . . .

. . . Or get all dressed up.

Before you realize it, you'll be an expert PugTherapist who understands that no matter which way you turn, you're always on the road to somewhere.

And no matter where you wind
up, there will be games to play...

Seasons to celebrate . . .

gardens to plant . . .

new friends who are
completely different
from you . . .

and old friends who are
just the same . . .

faith . . .

. . . and lots and lots
of cuddling.

Best of all, you'll realize
that while there is great strength
in numbers ...

. . . you can always count
on you.

The End

Acknowledgments

We would like to thank our editor, Ann
Campbell, for her elegance and her enthusiasm,
not to mention her generosity in lending us
Elvis's soul brother Merlin; Ursula Cary for
her sense of fun and the best puppy treats in
town; and our agent, Jenny Bent, a true original.
A very special thank-you to our cover pug par-
ents, Kim and Bill Puccio, and their adorable
pug, Lola Jean, who stole Elvis's heart and ours;
to Tonya Chen and Ben Mezrich and their

incomparable pug, Bugsy, the best-dressed pug in this or any other town; and to Kristen Kreft for being such a great mom to our long-lost puppy, Busta. And of course, we want to thank our own Elvis Ramon, who is, in our eyes, the cutest and the wisest pug in the whole wide world.

BEV:

Thanks to my two-legged family: Ellen Rees and David Oldes, Marilyn and Bill Knox, and Tod, Carra, and Jake Knox. Thanks also to my family on four legs: Elvis, Daisy, Bert, Buddha, and Hamlet. A very special thanks to the soon-to-be-world-famous Jessica Alonso for her unerring eye, awesome talent, beautiful spirit, and generous heart. And of course, to my one and only Jason, who brought pugs and so much more into my life the night he came to dinner and never left. I love you, baby! The best is yet to come.

JASON:

I would like to thank my zany family: John, Darlene (Big D), James, and J. P. Bergund; Lee, Teesh, and Richelle Thoburn; and my Stella "Ole Woman" Holden. I'd also like to thank my friends for filling our home with love and laughter. A big thanks to my favorite Georgia peach, Jessica Alonso; I continue to be in awe of your shutterbug talent. I treasure our friendship and love you very much. Thank you also to the greatest dogs in the world, our own Elvis, Daisy, Bert, and Buddha, and that #*&*! cat, Hamlet. Last but not least, thank you to my number-one girl, Bev West. I love you more than any words could express, and I hope our amazing journey together never ends.

JESSICA:

I would like to thank my family for their unwavering support. A special thanks to my mom, Connie Alonso, who made me an avid animal lover and got me my first pet, Maggie the Cow; to my sister, Jennifer Alonso, for giving me my first camera; and also to Ronnie Kittrell. Much thanks to all of my friends who have encouraged me in my creative endeavors. Also, thanks to Bruce Habegger for his expert eye, and thanks to Samantha and Charlie Mozes for their laughter, inspiration, and use of their "car." Most of all, thanks to Bev West and Jason Bergund for inviting me to join them on this wonderful journey. May it never end. I love you both!